# POP CLASSICS FOR TWO

Arrangements by Mark Phillips

ISBN 978-1-5400-6537-7

Visit Hal Leonard Online at
**www.halleonard.com**

Contact us:
**Hal Leonard**
7777 West Bluemound Road
Milwaukee, WI 53213
Email: info@halleonard.com

In Europe, contact:
**Hal Leonard Europe Limited**
42 Wigmore Street
Marylebone, London, W1U 2RN
Email: info@halleonardeurope.com

In Australia, contact:
**Hal Leonard Australia Pty. Ltd.**
4 Lentara Court
Cheltenham, Victoria, 3192 Australia
Email: info@halleonard.com.au

# AFRICA

TROMBONES

Words and Music by DAVID PAICH
and JEFF PORCARO

Play 3 times

To Coda

2nd time, D.S. al Coda
(take repeats)

CODA

# ALONE

TROMBONES

Words and Music by BILLY STEINBERG
and TOM KELLY

# CAN'T SMILE WITHOUT YOU

TROMBONES

Words and Music by CHRIS ARNOLD,
DAVID MARTIN and GEOFF MORROW

# CENTERFOLD

TROMBONES

Words and Music by
SETH JUSTMAN

**Moderately**

# DANCING QUEEN

TROMBONES

Words and Music by BENNY ANDERSSON,<br>BJÖRN ULVAEUS and STIG ANDERSON

# DUST IN THE WIND

TROMBONES

Words and Music by
KERRY LIVGREN

# EVERY BREATH YOU TAKE

TROMBONES

Words and Music by
STING

D.S. al Coda

CODA

# EYE OF THE TIGER

Theme from ROCKY III

TROMBONES

Words and Music by FRANK SULLIVAN
and JIM PETERIK

# I MELT WITH YOU

TROMBONES

Words and Music by RICHARD IAN BROWN,
MICHAEL FRANCIS CONROY, ROBERT JAMES GREY,
GARY FRANCES McDOWELL and STEPHEN JAMES WALKER

**Moderately fast**

# I STILL HAVEN'T FOUND WHAT I'M LOOKING FOR

TROMBONES

Words and Music by
U2

# IMAGINE

TROMBONES

Words and Music by
JOHN LENNON

# JESSIE'S GIRL

TROMBONES

Words and Music by
RICK SPRINGFIELD

**Moderately fast**

# LEAN ON ME

TROMBONES

Words and Music by
BILL WITHERS

# PIANO MAN

TROMBONES

Words and Music by
BILLY JOEL

# RIGHT HERE WAITING

TROMBONES

Words and Music by
RICHARD MARX

# SILLY LOVE SONGS

TROMBONES

Words and Music by PAUL McCARTNEY
and LINDA McCARTNEY

# THE SOUND OF SILENCE

TROMBONES

Words and Music by
PAUL SIMON

# STAND BY ME

TROMBONES

Words and Music by JERRY LEIBER,
MIKE STOLLER and BEN E. KING

# SWEET CAROLINE

TROMBONES

Words and Music by<br>NEIL DIAMOND

2nd time, D.C. al Coda

CODA

# TAKE ON ME

TROMBONES

Words by PAL WAAKTAAR
and MAGNE FURUHOLMNE
Words by PAL WAAKTAAR,
MAGNE FURUHOLMNE and MORTN HARKET

*(small notes optional)*

# TIME AFTER TIME

TROMBONES

Words and Music by CYNDI LAUPER
and ROB HYMAN

# WE BUILT THIS CITY

TROMBONES

Words and Music by BERNIE TAUPIN,
MARTIN PAGE, DENNIS LAMBERT
and PETER WOLF

# YOU ARE SO BEAUTIFUL

TROMBONES

Words and Music by BILLY PRESTON<br/>and BRUCE FISHER